RUBANK EDUCATIONAL LIBRARY No. 36

RUBANK Elementary METHOD

Eb or BBb BASS
(TUBA - SOUSAPHONE)

N. W. HOVEY

A FUNDAMENTAL COURSE FOR INDIVIDUAL
OR LIKE-INSTRUMENT CLASS INSTRUCTION

RUBANK®

HAL•LEONARD®
CORPORATION
7777 W BLUEMOUND RD PO BOX 13819 MILWAUKEE, WI 53213

Fingering Chart for Basses

(see footnote)

N. W. HOVEY

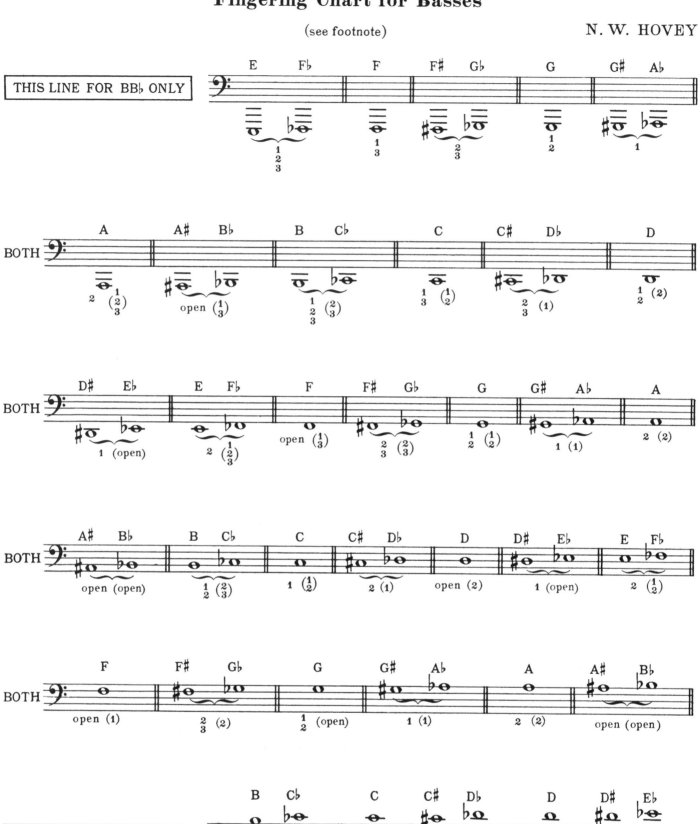

In this chart and under each new note introduced in the following lessons will be found the fingering for both BBb and Eb Bass. The BBb fingering is indicated first, followed by the Eb fingering in parenthesis.

Whole Notes and Rests

N.W. HOVEY

Half Notes and Rests

Half Notes and Rests

Quarter Notes and Rests

Quarter Notes and Rests

see footnote

5

(E♭)

1 (open)

The sign ⅍ indicates that the preceding measure is to be repeated.

Key of E♭

Note: All exercises previous to this lesson have been in the Key of B♭ in which B and E are flatted. This lesson introduces the Key of E♭ in which B, E, and A are flatted. Form the habit of looking at the key signature before you play each exercise in the following lessons.

The Tie; Dotted Half Notes

Practice softly. Learn to conserve the breath so as to get maximum tone with minimum effort. Practice daily on slow, even, sustained tones.

Three Quarter Time

The sign ♮ is called a "natural". It cancels the effect of the A flat in the key signature, for one measure only. Occasional sharps, flats or naturals not appearing in the key signature are called "accidentals."

Eighth Notes

Rhythmic Patterns to be practiced. Repeat each several times.

(abbreviation)

open (1)

Turn to page 44, no. 1, 2 and 3 for melodic material.

Eighth Notes

< or crescendo (usually abbreviated cresc.) gradually louder.
> or diminuendo (usually abbreviated dim.) gradually softer.

Eighth Notes

14

Key of F

(one flat — B)

Note that key signature calls for B flat *only*.

Dotted Quarter Notes

Rhythmic Patterns to be praticed. Repeat each several times.

*Be certain before proceding with lesson 14 that you can recognize and define the Key Signatures you have had thus far, (namely, F Bb and Eb) and have *memorized* the three major scales.

Dotted Quarter Notes

Turn to page 44, no. 4 and 5 and page 45, no. 6 and 7 for melodic material.

Eighth Rests

Rhythmic Patterns to be practiced. Repeat each several times.

LESSON 16

Eighth Rests

Key of C
(no flats or sharps)

If you have memorized four major scales (C, F, B♭, E♭) procede with the next lesson; if not, review lesson 18, No.1, Lesson 13, No.1, Lesson 14, No.7 and Lesson 7, No.1.

LESSON 18

The Slur

Alla Breve (cut time)

Alla Breve

Alla Breve

Play lessons 4, 5, 6 and 7 in ¢ for additional practice.

Key of A♭⋆

(four flats—B, E, A and D)

⋆) After completing this lesson the pupil should be able to play 5 major scales from memory,(namely C, F, B♭, E♭ and A♭).

Six-Eight Rhythm

Practice each of the following 6-8 lessons beating *six* to a measure emphasizing or slightly accenting counts 1 and 4, (1 2 3 4 5 6). Then review each lesson beating *two* to a measure, so the first beats falls on count *one* and the second beat on count *four*.

(1 2 3 4 5 6)
(1 - - 2 - -)

Six-Eight Rhythm

Six-Eight Rhythm

Turn to page 46 no. 9 to 12 for melodic material.

Key of D♭*

(five flats — B, E, A, D and G)

*) After completing this lesson the pupil should know six major scales from memory, namely C, F, B♭, E♭, A♭ and D♭.

Sixteenth Notes

(see footnote)

Number 1 is a rhythmic exercise. Play both lines and compare. Notice that any eighth note may be replaced by two sixteenths. Invent some rhythmic patterns of your own.

Sixteenth Notes

Sixteenth Notes

(abbreviation)

(Review no. 5 using articulations above.)

Key of G♭★

(six flats—B E A D G and C)

refer to
lesson 27

★) After completing this lesson the pupil should know seven major scales from memory. (Namely, C, F, B♭, E♭, A♭, D♭ and G♭)

Dotted Eighth Notes

Dotted Eighth Notes

Turn to page 47 for melodic material.

Additional Rhythms in Alla Breve

Play lesson 14, no. 1 in ₵.

Key of G ⋆

(one sharp—F)

⋆) After completing this lesson the pupil should know eight major scales from memory.(Namely, G,C,F, Bb,Eb,Ab,Db and Gb)

Chromatic

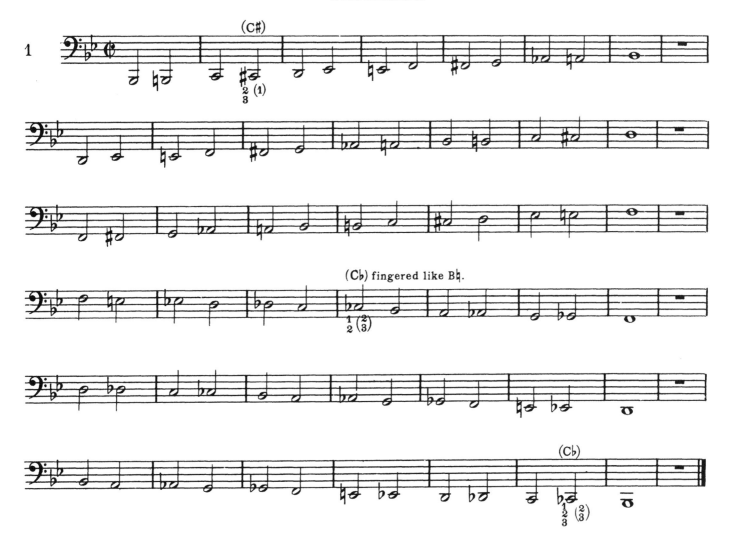

In the following exercise, breathe deeply, play slowly. Keep the crescendo and decrescendo even. Each line should take but one breath.

Chromatic

Key of D⋆

(two sharps—F and C)

⋆) After completing this lesson the pupil should know nine major scales from memory (namely D, G, C, F, B♭, E♭, A♭, D♭, and G♭).

Syncopation

Be certain the accent is on the correct note. A common error is committed in playing syncopated figures as follows:

Incorrect

tu tu *ah* tu

Syncopation

Triplets

In previous lessons you have divided the quarter note into two equal parts (♩ = ♪♪) and into four equal parts (♩ = ♬♬) It may also be divided into three equal parts.

Be certain you play each of the notes in the triplet figure, with equal value. A common error is committed in playing the figure in this way ♫♩. Do not rush the first two notes.

Intervals

These exercises should be practiced in two ways. First, starting each note with a definite attack and second, slurring from the first note to the second.

Turn to page 48 for melodic material.

Scales for Reference

Melodic Material

Doxology

Duke Street

Abide With Me

WM. H. MONK

Blue Bells of Scotland

Scotch Folk Song

Adeste Fideles

Traditional

In the Gloaming

A. F. HARRISON

O Canada

C. LAVALLEE

America the Beautiful

SAMUEL A. WARD

Drink to Me Only With Thine Eyes

Andante Moderato

English Air

Sweet and Low

Larghetto

J. BARNBY

The Old Oaken Bucket

Andante

S. WOODWORTH

It Came Upon a Midnight Clear

Moderato

RICHARD WILLIS

The Minstrel Boy

Irish Air

Love's Old Sweet Song

J. L. MOLLOY

Rocked in the Cradle of the Deep

J. P. KNIGHT

Old Folks at Home

STEPHEN C. FOSTER

In Happy Moments

WALLACE

Scenes that are Brightest

WALLACE